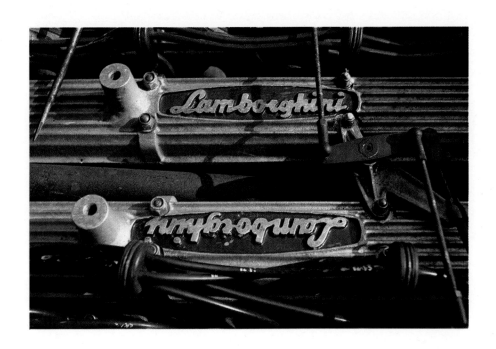

D1566089

Osprey Colour Series

LAMBORGHINI

SUPREME
AMONGST
EXOTICS

Andrew Morland

Published in 1985 by Osprey Publishing Limited
12–14 Long Acre, London WC2E 9LP
Member company of the George Philip Group

© Copyright Andrew Morland 1985

This book is copyrighted under the Berne
Convention. All rights reserved. Apart from
any fair dealing for the purpose of private
study, research, criticism or review, as
permitted under the Copyright Act, 1956, no
part of this publication may be reproduced,
stored in a retrieval system, or transmitted in
any form or by any means, electronic,
electrical, chemical, mechanical, optical,
photocopying, recording or otherwise, without
prior written permission. All enquiries should
be addressed to the publisher.

British Library Cataloguing in Publication Data
Morland, Andrew
    Lamborghini.—(Osprey colour series)
    1. Lamborghini automobile—Pictorial works
    I Title
    629.2'222   TL215.L33
ISBN 0-85045-654-1

Editor Tim Parker
Designed by Norman Brownsword
Printed in Italy

Contents

Introduction

Lamborghini – Supreme amongst exotics as a title for a book hardly needs to be justified but just in case there are some enthusiasts who might want to argue, here's a short consideration. In fact, it's a useful way to introduce this unique book, almost certainly the first and only wholly photographic work on the marque, and certainly that in colour.

Amongst those who discuss exotic cars it is generally accepted that there are only two names which truly vie for the top of the tree. Exotic cars are, of course, not the same as high performance cars nor even collectible cars. The word 'classic' used to describe a type of car won't even be considered. To be exotic the car must be rare, expensive, probably of middle European origin, very beautiful—either ultimately or technically (and preferably both) and simply downright desirable. One can assume also that the car must be fairly modern—if not other descriptions than exotic seem to be in vogue.

The two marques are thus Ferrari and Lamborghini. For Lamborghini the points mount up this way: very small numbers made—almost certainly no more than 5000 examples in total. Always expensive, usually very stylish, always either V12 or V8 powered, sometimes mid-engined, and often with unpronounceable names. Ferrari, on the other hand, are indeed more numerous—how many 308 Ferraris have been built?—expensive but not relative to a Lamborghini, and probably due to their racing successes and the involvement of Fiat, no longer

that unfamiliar. If you ask yourself when you last saw a Lamborghini on the street. Then a Ferrari?

Exotic-ness also involves quirkiness, to a certain extent the soundness or otherwise of both the manufacturer's business and the reliability of the cars themselves. See, now, how Lamborghini wins.

Finally, we should not dismiss Lamborghini's trump car(d)—the Countach. Surely 'the' exotic car, the pinnacle.

Within these pages we present every major Lamborghini production model plus some factory build shots and some just for fun. This is not, however, a catalogue of every car nor a collection of technical specifications. For those in need Osprey Publishing offers individual titles on each of the major models.

Photographer Andrew Morland, one of Britain's best known automotive photographers offers his thanks to the following who helped him with this work: David Joliffe of Portman Lamborghini, George Street, London W1 who loaned two cars for action photography, one driven ably by Alex Postan and the other entrusted to Tim Parker. Patient camera car drivers were Virginia Allan and Helen John. Ray Beverley of the British Lamborghini Owners' Club was enthusiastic as were the following owners—Peter Hampton, Peter Oates, Colin Earl, Nicholas Portway, Ivor Halbert and Mr P. Berry. Dick Clarson of Graypaul Motors near Loughborough gave us time with a Miura in his charge after his company's restoration.

1 **Only the lonely**

Right This photograph and the next four are all of the same car at the factory, taken in April 1984. This particular car, a Countach 5000 S, destined for an Italian was being road tested prior to final cleaning for collection by the customer. In between the rain, the test driver, topped up fluids, adjusted linkages and generally tidied everything. There was no urgency in any of his work, just calmness and obvious intent to get the car right. Great care was being taken.

To the left of the photograph is the main door to the production line. In the far right is reception and the works dining room. Neither building seems to have been either decorated or modernized since being built and the atmosphere is one of careful, almost calculated work.

Overleaf The Countach, the 5000 S is the model just prior to the latest Quattrovalvole, with covers open. For the test driver, just everyday, for us perhaps much more

Interesting shot of the Countach looking over to
the factory's service and maintenance department
with the factory's road test Jalpa, just back from
Italian press duty, alongside a mid-fifties Bentley S1
Mulliner convertible awaiting some restoration.
The factory don't just repair their own products!

Right Countach interior. Its style certainly in keeping with the car's exterior. Anyone who's ridden in a Countach will know how gripping those seats need to be

Below From the rear is the normal view for most Countach spotters as the car blasts by. Just superbly aggressive. The near door is to the production line end, the far is where it all starts with chassis and body panel construction

13

Jalpa, today's other Lamborghini. Like the Countach its current bodyshell design has been developed from something not quite the same, although unlike the Countach, this one is pretty far removed from the original, the Urraco P250 in 1972. Obviously the Countach of 1971 was right to start with

The Jalpa is the affordable Lamborghini but undoubtedly suffers under the shadow of the Countach, simply because the Countach is so radical and so exotic. Jalpa drivers all tell of the same excellent road manners

2 Hand crafted for the few

Right Main gate to the factory. Visitors park on the left, customers and road test cars, and obviously trucks with components, to the right. Behind the Lamborghini sign is the works canteen. It always seems to rain . . .

Below Village sign. If you didn't know it was there, the Lamborghini factory that is, you would pass through S. Agata Bolognese at 50 km/h and without blowing your horn. Sant'Agata is twinned with Laktasi in Yugoslavia

That fabulous tubular steel Countach chassis, cut, tube bent and welded outside the factory. Rear 'wings' on travelling jigs await alongside. Chassis comes painted black

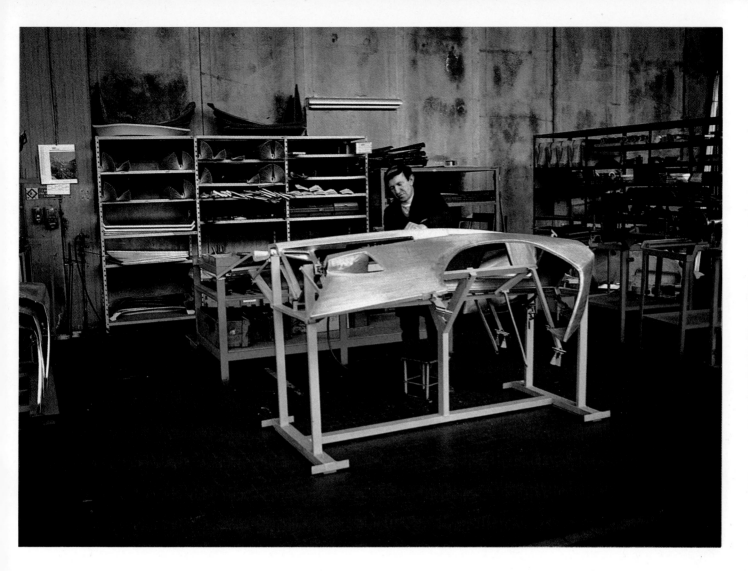

Above Panel rolling and beating is all done in house and mostly by hand. Here are some Countach 5000 S rear wings being finished prior to bodyshell mounting

Overleaf The coming together of Countach chassis and body panels takes place in this jig. Careful welding ensures reasonal accuracy. *Inset* Final fettling prior to painting for the rear boot lid. Note the fibreglass wheelarch extensions, the need to cut out the rear lamp housing and the brown 'paper' insulation

Two Countach chassis/bodyshells completed but without filling, rust protection or primer. The whole thing is mighty strong, make no mistake, but it's possible to see why such a car is difficult to maintain, repair let alone restore

Above Lamborghini's de-rusting booth in which the inside and out of their bodyshell is coated with protective sealant, in their case, it's green. Once more, everything is done by hand

Overleaf Jalpa's turn. The Jalpa bodyshell comes in virtually complete by road from Bertone, in Turin. A line of them wait on dolleys after factory primer. Inset More hand finishing, after Jalpa spraying

Left Jalpa headwork. Air tools carefully worked by hand are used on every cylinder head even after the computerized machine tools have done their best

Below Piles of Countach cylinder heads and Jalpa camdrive end covers proliferate. Countach blocks are being checked on that flat engineer's table. Batch testing is regularly done

Overleaf Countach production line was busy, at least in April in 1984. Here a workforce of as many women as men fit out the cars. *Inset* Door finishing. Aluminium panelling such as this can take hours of work to reach this stage

Right and below The Countach power train is a mighty object. Cylinder heads await finishing and valve fitment, and engine comes together. This one awaits heads. Note the differential housing to the right

The car's nearly finished and lunch is not far away.
Hours and hours are spent in fitting the electrics,
pipework and the headlamps; special sealer is used
to make them work. Any number up to about five
people can work on one car at this stage. The
factory is clean and well lit

Finished, well not quite. Close to the end of the production line is the final tuning or fettling area. Here cars are adjusted until they are right. Road testing takes place on every one—teeming rain or lengthy work brings the car inside here

Now finished. Completed cars, one Countach, the rest Jalpas await delivery or customers to collect. Many customers take great pleasure in visiting the factory to collect their new cars

For all to see, if they look, are some historic cars.
Close to the collecting area for new, finished cars
is this line of 'wrecks'. The yellow car is a crudely
modified Urraco with an unknown history, the red
car, on the other hand, is important. It's the
Urraco 'Bob' or Rally. Early test engineer New
Zealander Bob Wallace modified a P250 in 1973
with a fully blown 310 hp 4-valve 3-litre engine
almost to full Group 5 specification. Various things
were tried including a tall rear wing, Jota wheels
and front air dam and quite obviously the car went
fast. One day it may be restored

3 Maintenance takes courage

Right . . . and money. Lamborghinis are both difficult and expensive to maintain but soon become ruined if all is neglected. This is inside their maintenance facility. In the foreground is a lovely Espada Series 2. In the background, a Miura and a Chevrolet Corvette that was reported to belong to one of the two Mimran brothers, owners of the company

Overleaf Very busy with two Countaches, two Miuras and two Espadas in view. What makes better sense than to have your car serviced at the factory which built it, possibly even by the same staff who actually built it

Above Miura with the rear bodywork removed to gain access to the engine and transmission. Note the close proximity of everything

Right Two 350 front-engined Lamborghinis in seemingly excellent condition being fettled. These cars are now rare and are essentially differentiated from the later 400 by the single headlamps

Miura *sans* paint. This one looks suspiciously Jota-like because of the lip under its nose and the exposed Monza filler. What is it? Yet another good reason to visit the Lamborghini factory—there's always something special lurking around somewhere

Above Very rare 350GT Convertible or 350GTS. Only three or four of these cars were made, more's the pity

Right V8 power train removed and awaiting work, complete with 'rear' axle and exhausts. Once again note compactness

4 The first V12s – 350 and 400

The very first Lamborghini prototype had hidden flip-up headlamps and was called the 350GTV. The first production series, the 350GT, had a pair of unique oval headlamps which reportedly didn't perform well on the road in darkness! That's the reason why the 350GT featured on these pages doesn't have the 'proper' units fitted, instead making do with a factory conversion to the double paired round headlamps of the later 400GT.

Peter Hampton, of Sussex in England, bought this 350 new directly from the factory before there was an official importer in the UK. Apart from the headlamps, and an exchange Salisbury differential because of whine in the original, the car is virtually as it was in 1965 when purchased.

The car is faster than all reports suggest

Overleaf Beautiful sideview of Peter Hampton's 350GT showing off the classic lines of the Touring of Milan rewor'.ed Franco Scaglioni design first seen on the 350GTV first shown to the world at the 1963 Turin Show in October. Scaglioni was famous for his 'Bat' studies with Bertone.

The engine was designed by Giotto Bizzarrini with help from Giampaolo Dallara (who was also instrumental in the chassis design) and was a 3464 cc V12 with around 280 hp at 6500 rpm

Above From the rear one can easily see those four relatively small diameter exhaust trims. That 350GTV had six rear pipes. Lovely Borrani alloy triple knockoff alloy rims

Above and right The interior of this first production series Lamborghini featured high quality leather and the usual Italianate dashboard, steering wheel and transmission tunnel arrangement. The car's direct competitors were the Ferrari 250GT Lusso and the Maserati 3500GT, although the latter was only a straight 6-cylinder.

Rear passenger space was minimal, more 2+1 than 2+2. Here are the luggage straps. Peter Hampton still has the original fitted luggage itself that was more suited than people. Boot space must have been minimal

Above and right Nicholas Portway's lovely 400GT was first registered in January 1968, chassis number 01141, engine number 01139, and clearly shows off the minor external differences over those of the previous 350GT. Although the 350 and 400 are clearly sisters under the skin, actually each body panel is different in some way, with of course the rear screen being the most obvious.

This car is right-hand drive, too. The engine was overbored to 3929 cc with power now quoted at 320 hp

Overleaf The 350/400 series cars are rare. Exact figures are usually accepted as follows: 350GT, 120 examples; 350/400GT interim cars, 23 and 400GT, 250 examples. The interim cars were 350s with 4-litre engines and other detail changes—such as 400 headlamps. This ex-Beatle Paul McCartney car is one of the genuine 400s.

Above and left Dashboard detail on this right-hand drive car. Hand crafted in traditional materials but not, perhaps, in keeping with the exceptional style of the exterior. Close-up of the rev-counter exhibits an almost Art Deco appearance, way out of keeping with a late 1960's modern line for the rest of the car

Right and below 4-litre engine and a change in emphasis with the badging on the rear of the car. Perhaps if they tell the world it's a 2+2, it simply must be one!

Ferruccio Lamborghini is reported to have said that Jaguar's handsome twin-cam 6-cylinder engine was all one needed—a V12 wasn't actually necessary. How fortunate that he didn't heed his own words

Above Chrome air vent to the front of the windscreen. Note the name clearly cast in

Left Ivor Halbert's 18,000 mile from new 1968(?) 400GT, chassis number 1351, engine number 1645. Care should be taken in reading that special registration, LAM 1. For 'accurate' ignition he has converted it to Judson magnetos! Those quad headlamps came from Hella, whilst the 350GT's ovals were Cibie.

No one car is identical to the next in this series

5 For some still the Lamborghini — Miura

Simply beautiful Miura SV owned by Peter Oates and superbly restored by Graypaul Motors near Loughborough (usually known for their Ferrari work). For some enthusiasts still the most striking and technically interesting Lamborghini ever made

Left and below Important to an understanding of the Miura is the date when the first car was designed and built. The transverse, mid-V12-engined chassis was first shown to a stunned Turin Show in 1965. The body followed at Geneva a year later. This was a fantasy car when the norm was the Ferrari 275GTB: the V12 E type Jaguar and the Maserati Ghibli were still dreams

The chassis design had been the work of Giampaolo Dallara, with Paolo Stanzani, the body by Marcello Gandini for Carrozzeria Bertone. Prototype testing had been in the capable hands of Bob Wallace

Below The in-front driver dials were the traditional speedometer and rev-counter—over-revving that big 4-litre V12 would be both expensive and dangerous. The driving position doesn't suit tall drivers

Above Some parts of the Miura were conventional, like this centre instrument panel and exposed-gate gear shift, à la Ferrari. Every passenger needed the footrest to press upon when the full performance was being used

Above and right Miura SV means the last series, after the P400 and the S, dated around 1971/72. Approximately 150 of this last series were made, with 475 of the Miura P400 and 140 of the S. SV essentially meant the most developed chassis and engine with a quoted 385 hp

Performance was in keeping with the style of the exterior. Several contemporary road tests quoted top speeds in excess of 170 mph which was undoubtedly fast for its day. Acceleration was there to match although the brakes were usually criticised and most testers probably didn't get close to the point where the rear end might break away in fast cornering—something to be avoided with all that weight to control.

But as for style . . .

Overleaf Lovely angle of Peter Oates' Miura SV ably shows off those curious pop-up headlamps without the 'eyebrows' of the earlier cars, the top ones of which actually come up into the airflow attached to the headlamp rim when the lamps are raised. Actual headlamp lenses are at 45 degrees to the headlamp glasses. The SV's lack of eyebrows was a styling improvement. Note also the twin, almost horizontal 'vents', one of which housed the fuel tank filler. The radiator was front mounted with twin cooling fans behind

Lamborghini's bull. Certainly there's reason to suppose that founder Ferruccio wanted to visually challenge the might of the prancing horse of Maranello, home of his competitor Ferrari.

Body details were changed with the progress of Miura from the original P400 through the S series and thus to the SV. The SV was without its headlamp eyebrows plus a lower front grille and new side lamps and the rear wheelarches perhaps spoilt the original line a little because of their reprofiling to enable wider tyres to be fitted

NO ADMITTANCE

The original technical and styling design of the
Miura was unquestionably inspired by the Ford
GT-40. Giampaolo Dallara readily admits that he
saw the need for a mid-engined monocoque in the
general style of that famous Ferrari race track
challenger. These two photographs enable the
comparisons to be made, also showing how the
centre roof panelling formed the strength for the
whole for both front and rear bodywork just lifts
off complete

6 Espada – supreme amongst 4-seaters

Above and right Two Series 2 Espadas with late-type Jarama wheels at speed at Goodwood, in Sussex, during the 1984 Lamborghini Owners Club test day

Believed to be a Series 2 Espada—external differences were few and far between—although it cannot be confirmed without a better view of the interior

Above 1983 at Goodwood. The Espada is considered to be the most sophisticated genuinely high speed 4-seater with its excellent chassis and 4-litre, 350 hp V12 engine and 5-speed Lamborghini-built gearbox. It was a big car but it did its job well. Factory performance figures suggested 155 mph. With nothing really comparable on the market today potential businessmen are going by airplane and collectors are moving in on the 1217 examples built

Right The Espada design was influenced strongly by the Lamborghini show car called the Marzal. The Marzal's engine influenced the Urraco, the body design, the Espada. The Marzal was designed by Marcello Gandini of Bertone using a great deal of glass. With a Dallara designed semi-monocoque chassis the 400GT drive train incorporated much of what had been learnt. Two outside suppliers built first the chassis (Marchesi in Modena) which was shipped to Bertone in Turin for the body panelling

Left Moody shot at Goodwood in 1984. The rear panel of the Espada is certainly a carryover from the Marzal. It's glass just above the rear registration plate, doing nothing to hide what may be stored in the large rear boot, access to which comes from the inside. The car's a coupé not a hatchback

Above As the most successful Lamborghini model to date, in total numbers produced, that is, the Espada is relatively plentiful and still relatively inexpensive. Restoration or any kind of repair work is still costly, though, because whilst there are not actually 12 of everything, it appears that way

Above The standard Espada exhaust doesn't come in this V12 E type Jaguar style bunch under the centre of the rear of the car. Properly it should still use four pipes but they should be conventionally placed, two together at each side, and usually with the extractor trims.

Note the see-through rear panel

Right If the race track surface of Goodwood (this photograph shot in 1984) were the autobahn in West Germany then this Espada might feel happier. The Espada is not a track car, but would do well running from the rain at high speed across Germany—that's what it was good at

7 Sleepers? — Islero and Jarama

If the Miura was the start of a line of outrageous sports cars and the Espada was the conventional 4-seater GT car, then the Islero and subsequent Jarama were a continuation of Lamborghini's original theme, the 350/400GT. For some reasons unknown these two weren't terribly well received in their day, even though more than 500 were made between 1968 and 1978. Today, their value is being realised, and they are thus, sleepers.

Ivor Halbert's Islero 400GTS

Above and left This 1969(?) Islero 400GTS usually known as simply, an Islero S, was converted to right-hand drive by owner Ivor Halbert himself. Its chassis number is 6246, its engine number 2317. It's in superb condition having only done some 35,000 km

Right Another Islero S with headlamps up. This is Colin Earl's car

This lovely example is to German specification and was brought from the Lebanon to the UK for a certain amount of restoration. Major problem for current owners is that trim quality was lax at the factory during most of this build period. To be fair, there's more room in the back of the Islero than in the 400GT, but not much

The Islero shared virtually the same chassis as the 400GT but was overall longer, lower but of the same width. The Marazzi body is today considered handsome especially when complimented by the classic Campagnolo wheels. Its style is very much of the Mercedes-Benz roadster kind. The S had an uprated engine, 350 instead of the 320 of the first version, and a mildly redesigned chassis with lessons learnt from the Espada

Overleaf German specification cars had, amongst other things, non-eared knock-off centre lock hubs and that's why this car may appear slightly curious with British registration. Quoted speeds for the Islero were either 162 or 165 mph depending on what you read. The 400GT version was both lighter and quoted to be faster in spite of a less powerful engine

Jarama S from the rear at Goodwood in 1983.
Note the Miura style S on the rear panel.
Externally the Jarama S differs from the first series
version by having side wing vents just in front of
the door hinge pillars and a new style of road
wheel. The Jarama which superceded the Islero
was actually more Espada underneath than Islero.
Its track was that of the Espada but the wheelbase
was considerably shorter than either. Its looks,
though designed in house at Bertone, were farmed
out again to Marazzi for putting into metal.

   Also stunning performance was limited by too
much weight.

Above Barry Martina, current co-organizer of the
UK Lamborghini Owners Club, owns this stunning
blue Jarama S with later sunroof

Overleaf Busy enthusiasts study Martina's Jarama
at Goodwood in 1983. Background offers a
Countach alongside an Isetta bubblecar

These two photographs clearly show off some of the Jarama's qualities, and in particular those of the later S model. Firstly note those five-bolt wheels which were also eventually adopted on the late Espadas—these were an S fitment only. Also those front wing side vents—S only. Low, short and wide gives the Jarama a very aggressive line, couple that with the twin NACA ducts and the across front vent and the whole image appeals greatly.

The Islero and Jarama are indeed underrated

8 V8 is neat – Urraco, Silhouette, Jalpa

Right What should have by rights been a Porsche 911 and Ferrari 246/308 Dino beater, wasn't. The early Urraco couldn't stand the pace, although to be fair, it wasn't all their own fault. Today, they are beginning to be seen as highly desirable mid-engine sports cars. Transverse mid-V8-engine Bertone bodied Urraco was handsome and could be fast; build quality and delivery was suspicious.

   This is an early P250 model (because of its large double vent on the front panel) fitted with some later parts such as the road wheels

Overleaf Another P250 S dated 1974 owned by Mr P. Berry of Crawley, Sussex shot at Goodwood in 1984. The P250 made a quoted 220 hp from its 2463 cc double overhead camshaft V8. The S version offered no more power, just better interior equipment such as power windows

Above 3-litre Urraco—Urraco means a little bull— or Urraco 3000. Major external change is that six-louvre front panel; major internal change is the enlarged 3-litre engine with a quoted 250 horsepower. Build quality was much improved. This is a 1976 model, production having started in 1972 and stopped in 1977

Right Engine maintenance is difficult on all Lamborghinis, the Urraco is no exception. This shot clearly shows the closeness of the transverse V8 engine to the passengers' seat backs

Overleaf Detail close-up. Curious are the chrome-plated bumpers of this P300, at least at first sight, if one compares them with the earlier P250 and P300 shown here. In fact, they are correct. The other two cars have been retrofitted with the American specification black bumpers of the ill-fated P250 III, it would appear

Above Silhouette—rare beast indeed. Cruelly it could be called a Urraco P300 with a Targa top. Reality says something else. It was much more. First shown in March 1976 the Urraco 3000 had been restyled in a most aggressive style with new wheels, 'square' wheelarches, new rear side window treatment and an air dam. Only 52 cars were made

Right Urraco production ceased in 1979, Silhouette in 1978—the new Jalpa didn't arrive in the showroom until 1982. Three years of development there may not be in the Jalpa, but great car it is

The Jalpa runs a 3.5-litre version of the 90-degree double overhead camshaft V8—quoted 255 hp. Lovely road test car from the UK importer at speed and rest in Surrey: chassis number ZA9J00000 ELA 12150, engine number 12150

At least the interior now provides the passengers
with considerable comfort and some proper
degree of control with easy to read
instrumentation. The interior suits the exterior in
every way.

The Jalpa has the legs of a fuel injected 308
Ferrari Quattrovalvole in every way, and at last.
The original intention for the car was for this to
happen. It may have taken time, but the result is
well worth waiting for. The Jalpa is a well-
balanced, exciting car to drive and an easy car to
live with. A worthy V8 Lamborghini

9 Countach – the only word for it

Right The most outrageous production car in the world—the Countach. This one a 5000 S; S production started in 1979 after 160 cars had already been made between 1974 and 1977, the 5-litre engine came in late 1982. Location Goodwood 1984 at the Owners Club meeting. Clever gull wing style doors require clever mechanicals

Overleaf This one is a Countach S, a late second series S with colour coded rear wing and Bravo style wheels and P7 Pirelli tyres. The S still carried over the LP400, 3929 cc dohc V12 engine—5 litres came with the S 5000

Left 5000 S coming out of the chicane at
Goodwood. The 5-litre engine is actually 4754 cc
to restore the horsepower rating to a genuine 375
from the falling horses of the LP400 S at about
340. The car is unquestionably fast, but just how
fast no one report seems to settle. An acceptable
180 mph must be within bounds

Another 5000 S. Bodywork changes for this car
over the LP400 S are nil except for the 5000 badge
on the rear panel. Demand for these cars is still
high. To date 150 LP400s have been sold, as have
385 LP400Ss and 325 LP500Ss. A satisfactory figure
for everyone

Contrast between Countach LP500s designed by
Marcello Gandini at Bertone and Ferrari 308GTB
(behind) designed by Pininfarina. Both are classic
in their own rights, although the comparison may
not be strictly fair for the Ferrari was conceived to
sell at a much cheaper price and at a much greater
volume, also to travel at a different scale of speeds.

Countach rear wing is still an optional extra,
although one usually fitted

Above Fast and very slow, or should that read, very fast and very slow. Countach versus Isetta bubblecar. Irony at Goodwood in 1984

Overleaf Early LP400 Lamborghini Countach, essentially unaltered from that first car shown to the world in 1971 at the Geneva Show. Hailed as nothing short of fantastic but also as too futuristic to have any practical use. How wrong everyone was. One hundred and fifty of these early style LP400s were made between 1974 and 1977.

Pure line

The Lamborghini importer for the UK readily offered their LP500S for on the road photography. This deep, deep dark blue/black example caused great excitement wherever it went. The inset shot is of an acceleration run during which wheelspin was offered for a lot longer than one might think for such a heavy car. Fast they go—some quoted figures offer zero to 100 mph in something less than 13 seconds! That's a standing quarter mile in around 14

Left and below On the open road and around town—all shot in Surrey. Docile the car can be too, high speed driving and round town slowness both come easily to its mechanicals provided one remembers it's a large car. Chassis number ZA9C00500 ELA 12744, engine number 12744

Right and below Beautiful longitudinally mounted double overhead camshaft V12 is mid-engined but the gearbox is actually under the gear lever inside the cockpit, without pulleys or cables. A driveshaft goes effectively through the sump of the engine to the differential at the other end, to the rear of the car

Beautiful style and excellent workmanship—
supreme amongst exotics. Due now, the latest
Quattrovalvole. Even more exotic